MAIDSTONE
A Pictorial History

'St Mary and All Saints College at Maidstone in Kent', *c.*1780.

MAIDSTONE
A Pictorial History

Ivan Green

Phillimore

1988

Published by
PHILLIMORE & CO. LTD.
Shopwyke Hall, Chichester, Sussex

ISBN 0 85033 684 8

Printed and bound in Great Britain by
BIDDLES LTD.
Guildford, Surrey

To Margaret

List of Illustrations

Acknowledgements

I should like to record my grateful thanks to many people, and organisations, who have helped me in many ways, especially to: officers of the Kent Library Service, Mr. B. E. Bishop, Miss C. Dunn, Miss J. Monkton and Mrs. M. Waite, and especially to the Maidstone Reference Librarian, Mr. Brian Taylor; the Mayor and the Borough Council and its secretary, Mr. K. B. Rogers; the Mayor's marshal, Mr. Derek Marraner, a real enthusiast; the vicar of All Saints' church, the Reverend Canon P. A. Naylor, and to Dr. Robert Hardwick, Dr. Richard Stevens, Mr. Marlow, warden of the Cutbush Charity Almshouses, Mrs. Mary Stevens and Mr. Steven Carswell; and, most important, to the people who make a book out of an author's material, Mrs. Frances Mee and the staff of Messrs. Phillimore and Company, the publishers.

There are also many people who, over many years, have given or loaned me photographs, pictures and prints and who have given valuable information. I hope that they will know that they are not forgotten and that, unfortunately, some material has had to be omitted because of the nature and scope of the subject. To you all, thank you.

I wish to thank the following for permission to take, or copy and reproduce, illustrations in this book: The Kent Library Service for Nos. 4, 6, 30, 33, 35, 36, 42, 61, 73, 74, 77, 103, 105, 113, 120, 126, 147 and 159; the Maidstone Borough Council for Nos. 19, 21 and 22; the Reverend Canon P. A. Naylor for Nos. 43, 45, 46, 47 and 48; Mr. John Hartley for No. 60; Dr. Robert Hardwick for Nos. 67-69. The remainder are my own prints, or photographs taken over the past 30 years.

Historical Introduction

Maidstone, the county town of Kent, is situated in the centre of the county at the confluence of several main roads and a river crossing, near the edge of a huge prehistoric area of water now referred to as the Wealden Lake. It was on the northern shore of this lake that an iguanodon, a large animal three or four times the height of a man, died; its fossilised bones were discovered in a local quarry. The remains are preserved in the Natural History Museum in London and a representation of it is used as one of the supporters on the town's coat of arms. Remains of many other long-extinct animals have been discovered in the area, and the Maidstone Museum exhibits some of them.

With its sheltered valleys and dry uplands, early men found the area a desirable place in which to live. Within a short distance of the centre of the present town, evidence of the activities of Old, Middle and New Stone Age men has been found: their primitive stone tools and the knapping floors on which they fashioned them; their communal constructions using local sarsen stones, of which Kits Coty, the Countless Stones and the Addington Stones are examples, though their exact function is still open to some speculation. Bronze Age men, too, left evidence of their life here and Iron Age camps and earthen forts attest to their somewhat uncertain and precarious hold on the area.

The influence of the Romans is shown by the remains of their villas and their great road which stretched from Rochester to the south-east coast and of which the present Week Street and Stone Street are surviving parts. The Romans are known to have quarried the local ragstone and some believe there to have been a Roman station in the area.

The village appears to have been situated in the V-shaped junction of the tiny River Len and the Medway, but little is actually known about it. Casual finds indicate a continuous occupation throughout the Saxon period and Maidstone or Maegthanstane is recorded in the *Textus Roffencis* of A.D. 975 as being the property of the Archbishop of Canterbury, in which condition it remained until the dissolution of the religious houses in the 16th century.

Penenden Heath, north-west of the town, was the old shire's assembly-place and also the place of public executions until the 19th century. Hasted records the famous assembly there in A.D. 1076, when the Archbishop recovered from Odo, William of Normandy's half brother, church properties which he had illegally seized. Among the many distinguished witnesses was the old Saxon Bishop of Chester, 'an antient man, well versed in the laws of the realm; who on account of his great age was ... brought hither in a waggon'. Domesday Book also gives a good picture of the manor in 1086:

Maidstone. It answers for 10 sulungs. Land for 30 ploughs. In lordship 3 ploughs.
25 villagers with 21 smallholders have 25 ploughs. A church: 10 slaves; 5 mills at 36s 8d; 2 fisheries at 270 eels. Meadow, 10 acres; woodland, 30 pigs.
Of this manor 3 men-at-arms hold 4 sulungs from the Archbishop; they have 3½ ploughs in lordship, and 32 villagers with 10 smallholders who have 6 ploughs. 10 slaves. They (also) have 1 mill at 5s; meadow, 13 acres; 2½ fisheries at 180 eels; 2 salt-houses; woodland, 23 pigs.
Total value of this manor before 1066 £14; when acquired £12; now the value Archbishop's lordship £20; the men-at-arms' £15 10s. The monks of Canterbury have 20s from 2 men of this manor every year.

A sulung was a Kentish unit of land measurement, equal to approximately 200 acres. Maidstone was a manor of medium size, with a Saxon church, water mills, eel fisheries, salt-houses, meadows and a considerable acreage of arable land and woods. Such a manor was of course self-supporting, producing everything the community required and, in any case, lacking the money to purchase elsewhere. The little church was dedicated to St Mary and this building, or perhaps a late 11th- or 12th-century replacement, survived until the last decade of the 14th century when it was demolished and the present church built. Nearby was a modest house for the priest.

The 13th century saw many changes, although there was little improvement in the condition of the great majority of the people who continued to be dominated by the church at a time when many other communities had achieved, or were achieving, a degree of independence from medieval overlords, both ecclesiastical and civil. These places, such as the Cinque Ports, were prospering greatly.

In 1260 St Peter's church and hospital, called 'Le Newerk of Maystone' and dedicated to SS Peter, Paul and Thomas of Canterbury, was founded by Archbishop Boniface to give shelter to the large number of pilgrims, especially those using the ancient trackway now called Pilgrims' Way, which ran just to the north. In the following year, Henry III granted the right to hold a market and from that time onwards the village began to develop into the trading and commercial centre of the surrounding countryside, a function assisted by its position. A bridge was built over the little River Len and probably also the gatehouse behind. This building is now the Information Centre. In addition, a small building, later to form part of the Corpus Christi premises, was erected in what was then the northern part of the inhabitated area.

The first three-quarters of the 14th century were rather uneventful, but this was more than made up for by the 'Great Rebellion of Kent' in 1381, a struggle to obtain greater religious and social freedom and to cast off the bonds of feudal tyranny. It is associated with the name of Wat Tyler, who was very possibly a Maidstone man, and also with the teaching of John Ball, a priest who refused to conform to the established social order. His question, recited to the oppressed underlings of his time, was:

> When Adam delved, and Eve span,
> Who was thanne a gentilman?

John Ball was considered to be a very dangerous revolutionary and was locked up in the archbishop's prison in the town, from where he was released by Wat Tyler's men in order to take part in the great campaign. The rebellion was in fact a failure, but its effects were considerable and long-lasting. In the last decade of the 14th century, a great building programme was carried out. An earlier bridge over the Medway was replaced by a new stone one and the Pope gave permission to Archbishop Courtenay in 1395 to convert the old parish church of St Mary into a college consisting of a master and 24 chaplains and clerks. King Richard II granted a licence for the foundation of the college and for the absorption into it of the old college of Newerk and its incomes. In consequence, St Peter's church and hospital, which by that time seems to have fallen almost into disuse, was dissolved and the buildings became increasingly ruinous until the rebuilding and extension of the church itself in the 19th century. The old church of St Mary was destroyed and the great new church in the Perpendicular Gothic style was erected, which still survives today. It has been said that the king's famous master mason, Henry Yevelle, who was involved in many of the great building operations of the time including the Westgate and the great nave in Canterbury, was responsible for Maidstone's new church.

It is a fine building, although severe and plain when compared with other buildings of the same style erected elsewhere.

The nearby College of Secular Canons was completed in 1397 and, on Courtenay's death, the church was completed by his successor, Archbishop Arundel. John Wotton, whose tomb is in the church, was appointed the first master of the college in 1398. Arundel, having completed the church, also rebuilt the Archbishop's manor house next door. This tripartite group of buildings comprising the church, the College of Priests and the manor house, now known as the Palace, remain today the most distinctive survivors of medieval building in the town even though time, neglect and alterations have destroyed some parts of them.

The principal source of trade in this period was the hewing and transportation of the local Kentish ragstone. A writ issued in 1348 for Thomas de Tottebury, who was clerk of the great wardrobe of Philippa, Queen of Edward III (who built Queenborough Castle and gave her name to the town there), reads:

> to bring stone from all quarries in the County of Kent, by the towns of Maydenstane and Allesford on the coast of the water of Medwaye to the Queens Wardrobe in Cheapside.

The craft of bell-founding was also practised in the town by Stephen Norton, who worked between 1363 and 1381.

In the 15th century the quarrying and shipment of the local ragstone continued. In previous centuries the stone had been extensively used for major building work including many of the churches in Kent as well as buildings elsewhere, including the Tower of London, the Palace of Westminster and Hampton Court. A new use for the stone from these quarries was to make spherical stone shot for cannons. During the 15th and 16th centuries, in particular, large consignments of stone shot were shipped from the town's wharves, especially during the reign of Henry VIII who was an expert in the employment of gunnery in war.

Maidstone was at this time governed by a portreeve, assisted by 12 leading citizens. Before he could take up office, the portreeve had first to be approved by the Archbishop to whom he was responsible both for his own actions and for the pliant behaviour of the citizens towards the church and church authorities.

The town's commerce was controlled by guilds, of which records of six survive: the artificers, cordwainers, drapers, haberdashers, mercers and victuallers. Work undertaken by these occupational guilds included the hewing and transporting of ragstone; the digging and transportation of fullers earth for the processing of cloth; the shipping of large quantities of wood for building purposes and ship construction; some cloth-making, although on a much smaller scale than, for instance, at Cranbrook, which was the most important cloth centre in Kent; and the digging and transportation of the fine local sand, very much in demand for glass-making.

In addition the town was developing into both a market centre for the surrounding countryside and, because of its central position, the county town, as is suggested by an Act of Parliament in 1496 which granted to Maidstone:

> The custodie for the weights and measure, as to a place commodiously situate to serve the whole shire in that behalf.

The principal building operations of the time were the alterations and improvements carried out by Archbishop Morton to the Archbishop's manor house in the last two decades of the century. Much earlier, in 1422, a prosperous local citizen, John Hyssenden, 'installed 25 inhabitants – elderly discreet men – in a certain ediface, to be called Brethren Halle'. This developed into the Fraternity of Corpus Christi, the charter being granted in 1441. The fraternity was a non-monastic order, rather like a 19th-century friendly society and by 1474 it was recorded that it consisted of some 104 men and 20 women. Most of the members were local business people of some substance in the town. A large amount of additional building was necessary and much of it, including part of the cloisters, survived until 1740. The hall still survives today.

Maidstone again featured as a centre for rebellion in 1450, this time under the leadership of Jack Cade, in protest against the lot of the underprivileged, suffering the continuance of ecclesiastical domination and financial impositions. The protest was well organised but it, too, failed, although it helped to reinforce public opposition to the continued abuse of power under which so many under-privileged people continued to suffer.

Early in the 16th century Maidstone's population was a little over two thousand. As trade and commerce began to grow, so too did the variety of occupations in the town. In addition to the established crafts and trades already mentioned, new ones began to develop: those of the coppersmiths, cannon-founders, hammer-makers and builders and operators of mills. At this time, two wheat mills, one malt mill and two potcher mills were leased to a Mr. William Shelden. Many of these new craftsmen were members of the Guild of Corpus Christi.

A period of fundamental change was initiated nationwide with the Dissolution of the Monasteries by Henry VIII in the 1530s. In Maidstone the College of Priests was suppressed and its members were pensioned off. The master, John Leyffe (or Leffe), was granted a yearly pension of £48 16s. 8d., a sum which in those days would have made him a rich man for life, the 15 incumbents under him all receiving much more modest sums.

Unfortunately, the king often granted the many valuable properties to the gentry or to court hangers-on rather than handing them over to the local community. In the case of Maidstone, the College property was handed over to George Brooke, Lord Cobham, in 1549. The manor advowson and prison house, previously held by the Archbishop, were at first retained by the king and then granted to Sir Thomas Wyatt.

A great step forward in the civic life of the town was the charter of incorporation granted by Henry's successor, Edward VI, in 1548. This gave the town a mayor, elected yearly, and 12 jurats to assist him in the government of the town. Maidstone's first mayor was Richard Heeley. It was a great change from the older chief officer, the Portreeve, who had to be presented to and approved by the Archbishop. At last, after centuries of ecclesiastical domination, the town had a civil administration whose officers were responsible to the townsfolk themselves.

However, this progression towards greater liberty was abruptly halted with the accession of Queen Mary, known throughout Kent as 'Bloody Mary' because of the religious persecutions which blotted both her reign and the career of her archbishop, Cardinal Pole. Many good Kentish folk died in foul prisons or were burnt at the stake, the latter ghastly death being imposed in Maidstone on three men, three women and a blind girl, in 1557. The news that the queen was to marry the fanatical Catholic King of Spain prompted a major, but unsuccessful, uprising in 1554 led by local gentry, the principal figure being Sir Thomas Wyatt. Wyatt, with many others, was executed after suffering the usual barbaric tortures during interrogation. The queen seized back from him the property which he had been granted by his father, and also revoked the town's charter of incorporation.

Her reign, however, was fairly short and in 1558 both she and Cardinal Pole died, at almost the same time. Their unlamented passing proved to be the final act of the medieval world since the new queen, Elizabeth, was made of different stuff. One of her first acts, as she tried to undo some of the damage done in Mary's reign, was to restore to the town its charter of incorporation in 1559. Maidstone was also granted the right to send two members to Parliament, and the earlier rights to a weekly market and four annual fairs were confirmed.

Due to the Duke of Alva's persecution of Protestants on the continent, in 1567 Elizabeth allowed Dutch craftsmen to settle in Kent. Many Walloons came to Maidstone and set up several new industries including the cultivation of flax and the making of linen thread, industries which survived and prospered for many years. Another local industry which began to develop was the growing of hops, for which the county has now became famous. These Dutch refugees were given the old church of St Faith in which to hold their own religious services and the Palace lands, with other property which Queen Mary had confiscated from Sir Thomas Wyatt, were granted to Sir John Astley, whose family held them for many years.

During Queen Elizabeth's reign, there were periods of prosperity and of stagnation and poverty, but the overall trend was towards progress. The town's position was a strong one; as a port and as the market centre for the river valley and the surrounding fertile lands, it was a good site for the establishment of industries and crafts. Its ready access to the Thames estuary ensured its general prosperity, as can be seen in many records which list the manufacture of linen thread, tapestry, sackcloth, armour, gunpowder, tiles, bricks, leather goods, ship-building and the making of white and brown paper, the latter industry increasing as linen thread production declined and taking over many of the old water mills for paper production. Camden, in his *Britannia* published in 1586, described the town thus:

> ... and now the Medway hastes to Maidstone ... this is a populous and neat town and of great length. In the centre is a palace of the Archbishops of Canterbury, begun by Archbishop John Ufford and finished by Simon Islip. The other common goal [gaol] of this county is here, and the town owes many of its privileges to Queen Elizabeth, who appointed a mayor for its chief magistrate instead of the Portreeve which it had before – Here below Maistone a little river from the east falls into the Medway, rising Leneham.

Maidstone had developed considerably later than other similar towns due to its inability to escape from feudal authority. Despite this, the contrast between the town at the beginning and at the end of the century is striking. In this one century, the town had successfully escaped from the remains of the old, restrictive medieval world into a newer, freer and expanding modern world.

In spite of many problems, the growth of the town in the 17th century continued apace, so much so that in 1662 it was listed as one of the 35 most prosperous towns in the country. The main industries continued to be the hewing and transport of the local ragstone, brick and tile manufacture, the digging and transportation of fullers earth, paper-, thread- and cloth-making, and the transport of waterborne goods from the Weald and surrounding areas. By the middle of the century brewing had become increasingly important and the Lower Brewery was recorded in 1652 as consisting of 'One capital messauge, with brewhouse, two malthouses, barns and stables, and a meadow'. The owner, John

Sanders, was mayor of Maidstone in that year. In his diary, Samuel Pepys noted that he had witnessed flax being beaten but the trade was on the decline and, before the close of the century, many of the fulling mills were being converted for other uses, marking the general decline in cloth production.

The town had increased both in physical size and in population. Anti-clericalism was very marked, as was a lack of enthusiasm for the Stuart royal house, in particular for Charles I's belief in the Divine Right of Kings to govern. Consequently, during the Civil War, there was considerable support for the Parliamentary cause. In his duty as Clerk to the High Court, Andrew Broughton, a leading citizen who had twice been mayor of the town, read the death sentence to Charles I. During his mayoralty, he presented a mace to the council which Maidstone still treasures.

Disaster occurred in 1648 when General Lord Fairfax approached the town at the head of a Parliamentary army. The local defence force was largely untrained and was led by the local landowners Sir William Brockman of Newington, near Hythe, and Sir Gameliel Dudley, both incompetent and amateur soldiers, who adopted quite the wrong tactics. The obvious plan for the defenders was to exploit their local knowledge of the surrounding countryside to resist where and when it would be sensible to do so, and thus to conduct a war of attrition.

Instead, the local royalist forces were marched into the town itself, whose population had considerable anti-royal leanings in any case, and here they had to try to resist Fairfax's battle-hardened troops in hand-to-hand fighting in the streets, a battle the defenders were bound to lose. Gradually they had to give ground and within five hours it was all over and they were forced to surrender. It was a bloody encounter which cost more than 300 men killed and wounded, 1,300 prisoners, 500 horses and eight cannons, and which in the end achieved nothing. A further disaster was the Great Plague of 1665-6, in which over 500 townsfolk died.

Bearing in mind the town's history, it is perhaps not surprising that the established church was largely in the doldrums and that nonconformity was rife, even though much discouraged by the establishment. The Presbyterians, Congregationalists and Baptists, in particular, secured a firm foothold and many smaller independent sects flourished, many of them only briefly, to be replaced by others. By the end of the century, Maidstone had an increasingly prosperous citizenry, which had finally escaped from the domination of the church and king, was thriving in business, in firm control of its local affairs and independent both in thought and worship.

Fortunately, we have a picture of Maidstone in the record of the journeys of Celia Fiennes who came to the town in 1697. She wrote:

Maidstone is a very neate market town as you shall see in the Country, its buildings are mostly of timber worke the streets are large the Market Cross runs down the middle of the greate streete a good way, there being three divisions in it one good Cross for fruite another for corne and another for all sorts of things. 2 of which is built over for the Town Hall and publick use; there is also a large Goal [Gaol]; this streete, notwithstanding the hall and cross stands in the midst, is yet a good breadth on each side and when it comes to meete in one is very broad and runs down a great length, quite to the bridge cross the Medway, which is not very broad here yet it beares Barges that bring up burdens to the town; it seems to divide the town for beyond the Bridge are buildings whole streetes which runs along the river, there are very pretty houses about the town look like the inhabitants of rich men, I believe its a wealthy place, there are severall pretty streetes, this was Market Day being Thursday and it seemed to be well furnish'd with all sorts of commodityes and I observed there was a great quantety's of Leather but could not learn what particular thing was their staple Comodity or tradeing in, but in general it seemed to be like a little faire for the variety of wares tho' they told me that was not so full a Market as some dayes, because the Country people were taken up aboute their hopping so could not bring things to Market.

The 18th century was a time of rapid progress. Banking and business in general prospered and new industries were replacing the old. The manufacture of thread from locally-grown flax was still undertaken in 1714 but it was very much in decline, as was cloth production in general. More of the old fulling mills either fell into disuse or were converted for use in paper-making. This was the case with the old Turkey Mill which was rebuilt as a paper mill, under the control of James Whatman, and which produced some of the most famous high-quality paper in the world. Padsole Mill, however, was not modified until 1795. The growing and marketing of hops was prospering and fullers earth was still mined and shipped from Maidstone quays in 1744, when its price was quoted as being eight shillings per ton. The old staple industries of the hewing and transportation of ragstone, brick- and tile-making and paper manufacture, were paralleled by a considerable increase in market gardening. This was due to the fact that large numbers of London's gardens were being built over to cope with the city's growing population. In order to satisfy new demand, large quantities of fruit and vegetables were shipped to London from Kent by hoys, the maids-of-all-work of the shipping world. Their operation was greatly assisted when, by 1740, the River Medway became controlled by locks which regulated the depth of water. The appalling state of the roads, however, hampered land transport which almost came to a halt in the winter months and after heavy storms; the situation was greatly improved by the advent of the turnpike roads. The turnpike from Maidstone to Rochester was built in 1728, that to Wrotham in 1752, Tonbridge in 1765 and Detling and Key Street in 1769. The turnpike to Biddenden was completed in 1803, by which time Maidstone's population had exceeded eight thousand.

Many fine houses, some of which still survive today, were built by prosperous, mercantile families. One old county family, the Astleys, moved away from the area when the family sold the Old Palace to Lord Romney. The Astleys had owned the building since the mid-16th century.

The 18th century was notable for its acts of charity, in particular the setting up of almshouses for the sick and needy, for example those of Sir John Banks in 1700, Edward Hunter in 1757 and John Brenchley in 1789. A perceptive view of Maidstone is given by Daniel Defoe in his *A Tour Through the Whole Island of Great Britain, 1724-6*.

> This is a considerable town, very populous and the inhabitants generally wealthy; 'tis the county town and the river Medway is navigable to it by large hoys, of fifty to sixty tuns burthen, the tide flowing quite up to the town ... London is supplied with more particulars than from any single market town in England ... From the same county are brought hops and cherries ... also a kind of paving stone ... so durable that it scarce ever wears out ... Also fine white sand for the glass-houses, esteemed the best in England for melting into flint-glass ... Also very great quantities of fruit such as Kentish pippins ... which come up as the cherries do, whole hoy-loads at a time ... This neighbourhood of persons of figure and quality, makes Maidstone a very agreeable place to live in, and where a man of letters, and of manners, will always find suitable society ... so that here is, what is not often found, namely, a town of very great business and trade, and yet full of gentry, of mirth, and of good company.

The increasing importance of the town as an administrative centre resulted in a new charter being granted by George II in 1748, specifying that the town should have 13 jurats, one of whom should be elected mayor, and 40 inhabitants as common council men. Shortly afterwards, in 1762, the old Lower Court House and Brambles prison were demolished and the present town hall was built. The County magistrates, who were also able to use the building, contributed £500 towards the cost.

In 1731, the tall spire of All Saints' church was struck by lightning. The spire was burnt out, but fortunately the building was saved; the spire has never been replaced. The nonconformist churches continued to develop, the oldest surviving building being the Unitarian church near the Arcade, which dates from 1736. The father of William Hazlitt, the great essayist, was its minister for several years.

In the last decade of the century (1792-4), the principal thoroughfares were paved, drained and lit. Thus, the medieval squalor of old Maidstone had by now disappeared. During the 19th century, Maidstone's population expanded rapidly from approximately 8,000 to over 33,000, an increase of more than four times. This brought about a boom in the building of houses, many of them of modest size for the increasing numbers of working class residents.

It was also a time of greatly increased religious activity, when 26 places of worship were built by the principal denominations: 12 Church of England, five Baptist, three Methodist, two Congregationalist, one Roman Catholic and three other churches and chapels. Mention must also be made of the many short-lived groups, mostly evangelical, who used halls, private houses or other temporary buildings.

Concern for the sick was evinced by the opening of the West General Hospital in 1833 and the setting up of many Friendly Societies, a notable early example being the Kent United Friendly Society of Brickmakers. An advance in education was the laying of the foundation stone of the Girls' Grammar school in 1887, the year of Queen Victoria's golden jubilee. Another important event in that year was the handing over of the Archbishop's Palace to the Mayor and Corporation, after it had been bought by public subscription.

However, the greatest advances were made in the adoption of modern services. In 1821 John Gostling made an agreement with the Commissioners of Pavement for the lighting of the principal streets by gas and two years later, the Maidstone Gas, Light and Coke Company was formed. A full gas service for lighting and cooking was offered to private households from 1851 onwards. The supply of water, too, was revolutionised. In earlier times, water from springs at Rocky Hill was piped to three conduits, situated at the top, middle and lower end of the High Street. Additional terminals were later added. This was superseded by the formation of the Maidstone Waterworks Company in 1860, which built a pumping station at Farleigh. This pumped water to a reservoir built at Barming, supplying the town through underground pipes. In later years, both the demand for the service and the number of sources from which the water could be pumped, increased. The typhoid epidemic of 1897 was blamed on the water supplied by the company, but the source of infection was never irrefutably identified.

Considerable supplies of water were beginning to be used by commercial companies, especially the breweries. Ralph Fremlin started brewing in Maidstone in the mid-1800s and, towards the end of the century, the two firms of Style and Winch amalgamated to form Style and Winch Ltd., a particularly successful merger which resulted in the acquisition of several other Kent breweries.

One of the greatest hazards in towns at this time was the risk of fire. There were no safety requirements for buildings, nor any organised fire-fighting operations. In 1804, the Kent Insurance Company, which had insured many local houses and business premises against the risk of fire, bought two manual fire engines for their properties in the town and engaged fire-fighting crews. Several years later, in 1862, the Police Fire Brigade was set up and provided with a hose cart and standpipes with which to tap into the town's water supplies. This was followed, some ten years later, by a voluntary brigade working under council auspices.

Maidstone was by-passed by the first main railway lines, but in 1844 the South Eastern

Railway opened a line from Paddock Wood station, followed by another from Snodland and Strood in 1856. In 1874 the London, Chatham and Dover Railway extended its line from Otford to Maidstone East and, ten years later, this was extended further to Ashford, thus providing a good connection with the Channel ports.

The increasing road traffic was much inconvenienced by the 14th-century bridge over the River Medway, which was only 11 feet wide. It was widened by an additional 11 ft. 3 ins. and its arches were reduced from nine to seven. The bridge was rebuilt in 1808, 30 feet wide and with only five arches. Later, it too needed replacing and a new bridge (the older of the two present bridges) was designed by the engineer Sir Joseph William Bazalgette. It was completed in 1879 and, shortly afterwards, the old bridge was demolished.

By the second half of the century, industry was expanding, both in the number and size of new enterprises, such as the large Fremlin Brewery in Earl Street. Maidstone was also becoming an important administrative centre for the county, dealing with the increasingly complex local government, the extension of the banking system and the emergence of building societies and insurance companies throughout the county. The 20th century began with yet another great advance in technology: the introduction of electricity as a municipal enterprise. A generating station was built at Fairmeadow, where a steam plant was used to drive dynamos to produce direct current. The system used was that designed by Stevens and Barker and the opening ceremony was held in December 1901. It was Stevens, along with his partner Tilling, who produced the famous Tilling-Stevens electric buses. Lorries were also made in Maidstone for many years, becoming well-known both locally and nationally. In 1904, the first Corporation tram service was initiated, the pioneer route being from the town centre to Barming, the same route used by the first trolleybuses in 1928. The trams ran until electric traction was finally abandoned in 1967 when buses, which had first appeared in the town in 1924, took over all the tram routes. In 1911, the Maidstone and District Motor Services Ltd. was formed and their familiar green buses are still to be seen operating throughout the county and beyond. The constant increase in traffic made it necessary to widen the bridge and in 1978 a second bridge, just downstream, was opened. The construction of Bishops Way and the adoption of one-way traffic approaching the bridge was then made possible.

The growth of business and industry continued. Firms such as Foster Clarke Ltd. and Sharpes, the toffee makers, expanded rapidly, as did the Maidstone Brewery. Papermaking continued to prosper and several engineering concerns, especially the manufacture of agricultural implements, developed. Perhaps the most successful local venture was that of the Rootes brothers who, in 1912, produced their first Singer car and later set up the important Rootes Group.

The effects of the two world wars and the great depression were far-reaching and the first half of the 20th century brought with it great suffering for the citizens of Maidstone as well as trade difficulties for local businesses. However, recent trends suggest the stabilisation of local industrial and agricultural operations, continuing office development, and the growth of the service industry. The county town of Maidstone has emerged as a major financial and administrative centre, a far cry from its origins as a Saxon archbishop's hamlet.

The Plates

Old Maps

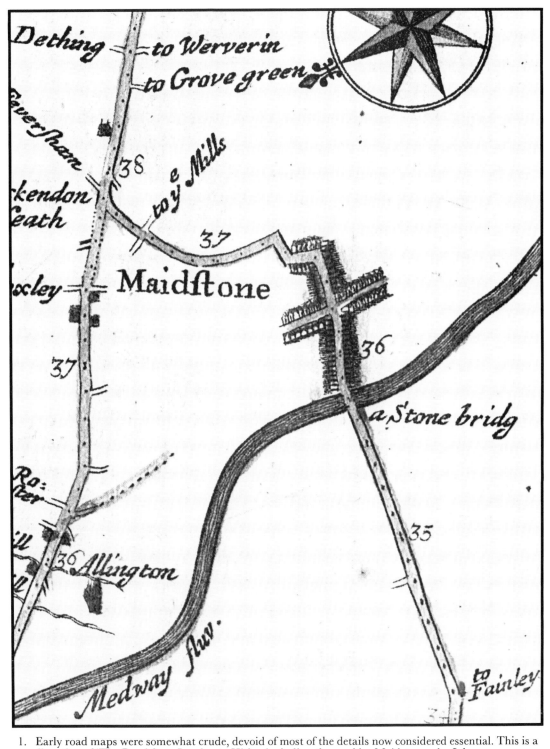

1. Early road maps were somewhat crude, devoid of most of the details now considered essential. This is a small section of 'The Road from London to Hith – including the road by Maidstone – by John Ogilby Esq.'.

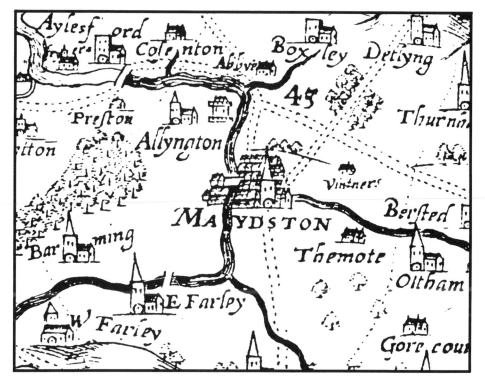

2. A section of Symonson's 'Map of Kent', 1596. Note that 'The Mote' and 'Vintners' were the important places on the outskirts of Maidstone at that time. All Saints' church can be seen with its tower and spire. In 1730 this spire, consisting of an oak frame covered with sheet lead, was struck by lightning and burnt, never to be replaced.

3. A small section of a map entitled 'The Hundred of Maidstone', published in Hasted's *History and Topographical Survey of the County of Kent*. The map was drawn in about 1798. All Saints' church is now shown without its spire. The road leading right from the bridge, now the High Street, is very wide since it was used as the market place. The surrounding area was largely rural and gardens. St Peter's church is shown, as is the Palace, but not the old College buildings.

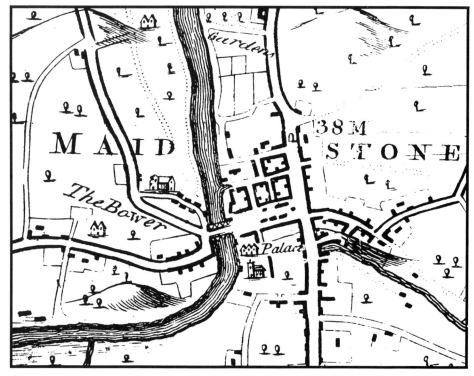

Old and New Views across the Town

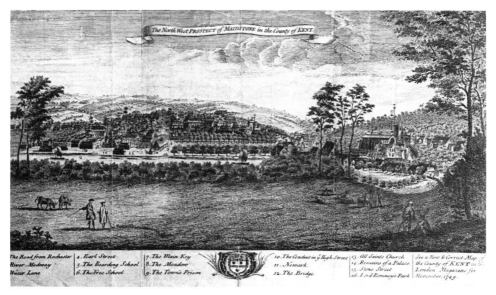

4. An 18th-century print of the town captioned 'The North West Prospect of Maidstone in the County of Kent'.

5. This fine picture of Maidstone across the river was probably produced in the second half of the 18th century.

6. 'Maidstone from Buckland Fields': an 1860s view.

7. This 1821 print of Maidstone from the south-west was drawn and engraved by I. Hawksworth, and shows All Saints' church with, to its left, the Archbishop's Palace and, to its right, the remaining buildings of the College of Priests. In the middle distance is the prison, completed two years earlier, in 1819.

8. 'Maidstone. From a field adjoining the London road', drawn by George Shepherd in 1830. At that time farm land stretched right down to the river bank, where sailing ships were moored. The stacked sheaves of corn indicate more leisurely farming techniques than those employed today.

9. This aerial view from the top of the Stoneborough multi-storey car park reveals the mixture of old and new building throughout the town.

10. In this modern view the tower of All Saints' can be seen at the centre.

The County Town

11. County Hall, designed by Mr. F. W. Ruck and built in 1915. It has an arched stone entrance, surmounted by a balcony, with pairs of classical pillars on each side supporting the top pediment.

12. 'The New Sessions House' was drawn by George Shepherd and published in 1829. The Sessions House was designed by Sir R. Smirke and erected about 1824.

13. 'The County Gaol', drawn by George Shepherd and published in 1829. The architect was Daniel Alexander and the grim building was constructed mainly of local Kentish ragstone.

14. The forbidding walls of the old prison, a great square which dominates the area behind County Hall.

15.   The present entrance to the prison, in County Road.

16.   A modern view of Penenden Heath, seen from the *Bull Hotel*. The heath was, from ancient times, the site of macabre public executions. Shire meetings, assemblies of the Kentish volunteer forces, and great political rallies were regularly held on the heath.

17. The County Library at Springfield includes this tower block beside the Chatham road.

18. The new Crown Court building on the opposite side of the river to the 14th-century church and Palace, and close to the south-west end of the bridge over the River Medway.

Municipal Maidstone

19. The new Maidstone coat of arms, photographed in 1988. The earlier dates of 1549 and 1949 which were suspended from the collars of the supporters have now been removed. These dates commemorated the granting of borough status to the town by Elizabeth I and the 400th anniversary of that event. The motto 'Agriculture and Commerce' sums up two of Maidstone's principal preoccupations, but the town's increasingly important role as administrative centre of the county is not represented. The supporter on the left is an iguanodon, the prehistoric remains of one of these creatures having been discovered locally, and that on the right is a lion rampant. The shield comprises the arms of Archbishop Courtenay, the creator of the College; the addition of the blue line represents the river flowing through the town. At the extreme top is the white horse of Kent, and round it a garland of hops.

20. Looking down the High Street from the drinking
fountain. On the left is the town hall. This was built in
1762/3 to serve both as the town hall and also as the
county magistrates court. The building houses many
treasures, including the town plate, two old tapestries and
several paintings, among them a portrait of Disraeli, who
first entered Parliament as the member for Maidstone.
Surprisingly, the dungeon is at the top of the building
instead of in the basement.

21. The fine late 18th-century staircase leading from the
front hall to the first-floor landing of the council chamber
in the town hall.

22. The well-maintained council chamber of the town hall in the High Street, a light and delightful interior with a decorated and coloured plaster ceiling, and restrained decoration on the flat wall surfaces between the windows.

23. A distinctive feature of the High Street is this prize from the Crimean War, a Russian gun, captured at Sebastopol and presented to the town in 1858. This drawing was made by Hugh Thomson in 1922.

24. The Russian gun occupies its island site in the High Street. Fortunately, it was not melted down during the Second World War.

25. A finial from the old Houses of Parliament, now in Brenchley Gardens. These gardens were presented to the town by Julius Lucius Brenchley in 1873.

26. The explanatory tablet attached to the old finial in Brenchley Gardens.

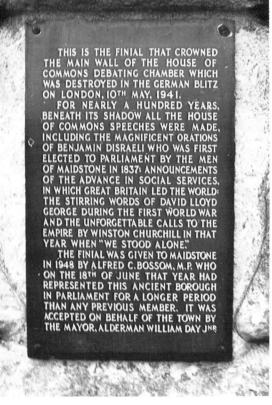

THIS IS THE FINIAL THAT CROWNED THE MAIN WALL OF THE HOUSE OF COMMONS DEBATING CHAMBER WHICH WAS DESTROYED IN THE GERMAN BLITZ ON LONDON, 10TH MAY, 1941.

FOR NEARLY A HUNDRED YEARS, BENEATH ITS SHADOW ALL THE HOUSE OF COMMONS SPEECHES WERE MADE, INCLUDING THE MAGNIFICENT ORATIONS OF BENJAMIN DISRAELI WHO WAS FIRST ELECTED TO PARLIAMENT BY THE MEN OF MAIDSTONE IN 1837: ANNOUNCEMENTS OF THE ADVANCE IN SOCIAL SERVICES, IN WHICH GREAT BRITAIN LED THE WORLD: THE STIRRING WORDS OF DAVID LLOYD GEORGE DURING THE FIRST WORLD WAR AND THE UNFORGETTABLE CALLS TO THE EMPIRE BY WINSTON CHURCHILL IN THAT YEAR WHEN "WE STOOD ALONE."

THE FINIAL WAS GIVEN TO MAIDSTONE IN 1948 BY ALFRED C. BOSSOM, M.P. WHO ON THE 18TH OF JUNE THAT YEAR HAD REPRESENTED THIS ANCIENT BOROUGH IN PARLIAMENT FOR A LONGER PERIOD THAN ANY PREVIOUS MEMBER. IT WAS ACCEPTED ON BEHALF OF THE TOWN BY THE MAYOR, ALDERMAN WILLIAM DAY JNR

27. Maidstone's one surviving water conduit has been removed from its original site and rebuilt as a wishing well on a new site near the east end of the museum and beside St Faith's Street.

28. The Market Building. These mid-19th-century pillars and arches form an arcade and a convenient walkway between the High Street and Earl Street, two of the town's shopping areas.

29. The Hazlitt Theatre, at the end of the Market Buildings and facing Earl Street, is named after William Hazlitt, the famous English essayist who was born in Earl Street in 1778.

30. Queen Victoria's Diamond Jubilee was celebrated in 1887 by the laying of the foundation stone for the Girls' Grammar School. The building was opened in 1888.

31.   The front of the museum and art gallery. A plaque reads: 'Opened as a museum and art gallery in 1858, the building has as its core Chillington Manor, the Elizabethan house of Sergeant-at-law Nicholas Barham, who acquired the estate in 1561'. The manor of Chillington is ancient, its records going back to the 14th century. Once part of the vast estates of the Cobham family, it passed to the family of Maplesden and so to George Maplesden who joined Sir Thomas Wyatt in the 1554 rebellion. In consequence, the estate was forfeited to the Crown, and in 1561 it was granted to Nicholas Barham. He and Henry Fisher became the first Members of Parliament for the town in the fifth year of Elizabeth I's reign.

32.   The Elizabethan front of the old manor house of Chillington is now somewhat overshadowed by large wings protruding on both sides. They were added in the last decade of the 19th century, the art gallery in 1890, and the College of Art in 1897.

33. A signed drawing of the front of the museum, art gallery and school, by the architect who designed them, Hubert Bensted.

34. This timber-framed addition to the rear of the museum was originally the old Court Lodge of East Farleigh, a few miles up river. It was dismantled and re-assembled here in 1874.

Buildings·in·connection·with·the·
CHARLES·MUSEUM·MAIDSTONE
Hubert Bensted ARCHITECT.

Ground plan

FARLEIGH
COURT
LODGE

35. Hubert Bensted's drawing of the rear of the museum buildings.

36. This interesting drawing of the rear of the museum, showing the re-assembled Court Lodge building, was made in 1922 by Hugh Thomson.

37. The public clock, near the new St Peter's bridge.

Churches

38. A 19th-century print of All Saints' church, looking from the south-east.

39. The size and commanding position of All Saints' church is well shown in this 1975 photograph, taken from across the river and looking to the east. Part of the old College is shown on the extreme right.

40. Good views of the church are difficult to obtain, because of the ill-advised planting of trees which grow too large over the years. This is the view from the south.

41. The great east window of All Saints' with, on the right, the smaller east window of the north chapel. The shallow roof pitches can be clearly seen.

42. This postcard of All Saints' church was produced *c*.1905.

43. The interior of All Saints' from the west. This Perpendicular Gothic church is generally dated to Archbishop Courtenay's time, c.1395. The chancel and sanctuary are certainly good examples of this period of building, but the nave is thought by some to be older. The font is not original. This font displays the arms both of Maidstone and of the Astley family who did not take up residence in the area until they were granted the old Palace after it had been returned to the Crown following the execution of Sir Thomas Wyatt in the 16th century. The late 14th-century font is now in Sevenoaks church.

44. The late 14th-century font which originally stood in All Saints' church.

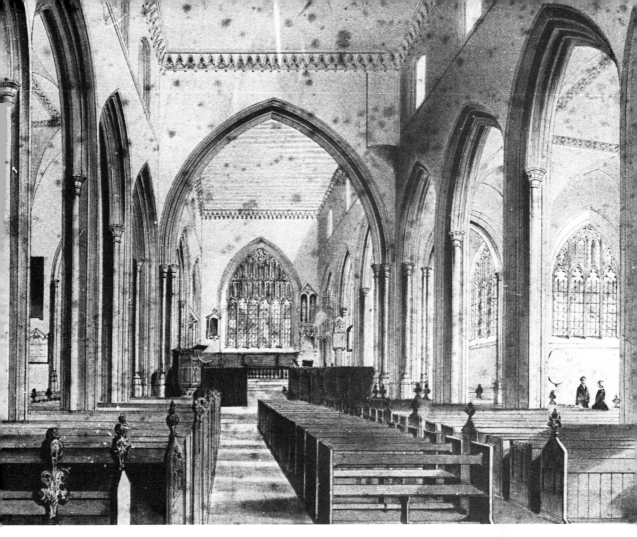

45. This beautiful 19th-century drawing of All Saints' church shows the fine proportions and great width of this plain but lovely building.

46. This picture was produced by J. Whichcord jnr., F.S.A., and published in 1849.

47. On the south wall of All Saints' church is this memorial to Lawrence Washington, who died in 1619. His arms, at the top, include the family stars and stripes, and a descendant of his, the famous George Washington, used this emblem as the model for the new flag of the United States. Many Americans come to All Saints' to see this memorial.

48. The Beale memorial. This is a sheet of copper, some thirty inches by eighteen, containing a record of seven generations of the Beale family. Each horizontal section represents a generation and is divided into three rectangles. The central rectangle shows the parents, the left rectangle the sons, and the right the daughters. The record begins with John Beale who died in 1399 and ends with Thomas Beale who married in 1593. The seventh generation is represented by another Thomas, son of the Thomas of the sixth generation, who erected the monument.

49. This mid-19th-century drawing is captioned: 'Maidstone Church. Wotton's Monument'. John Wotton was the first master of the College, and was buried in this tomb which he constructed in the south wall of the chancel in his own lifetime.

50. A 19th-century drawing of the fresco at the back of Dr. John Wotton's tomb. It is said to represent the Virgin Mary seated on a throne, and an angel presenting the soul of John Wotton (the small kneeling figure), pleading for exaltation to heavenly bliss. John Wotton died in 1417.

51. St Peter's church began life as a 13th-century hospital for travellers, founded by Archbishop Boniface, but its assets were transferred to the College of Priests when that institution was established in 1395. After centuries of neglect, the chapel of that old hospital was enlarged and re-consecrated as a parish church in 1837. The building, designed by Maidstone architect, Whichcord, is now redundant.

52. The statue on the side wall of the church is of St Peter with a cock, the bird traditionally associated with Peter and the passion of Christ.

53. Holy Trinity church in Church Street, *c*.1906. This building was designed by Whichcord in the classical revival tradition and opened in 1828. A most interesting building, it was constructed of the local ragstone for an original cost of £13,000. It is traditionally claimed to be one of 25 churches built to commemorate the Battle of Waterloo. It was renovated in 1875 but has long been redundant, the last service having been held there in July 1966.

54. Holy Trinity church in 1988. Efforts are being made to adapt the building for some kind of community use.

55. St Faith's church. The original building on this site was a chapel-of-ease, and it was lent to the Dutch religious refugees in the 16th century so that they could hold their own services. This old chapel was later demolished and the present church was built in 1872. This view is from Brenchley Gardens.

56. The Roman Catholic church of St Francis of Assissi, at the top of Week Street, near the County Hall.

57. The interior of the Catholic church of St Francis of Assissi.

58. The Unitarian church opposite the Market Buildings, the oldest nonconformist church in the town, was built in 1736 and has survived, little altered. For ten years, between 1770 and 1780, the father of William Hazlitt, the famous English essayist, was the minister, and William was born nearby. The family left Maidstone when William was still very young.

59. The Baptist church in Knightrider Street was built on the site of the earlier Bluecoat School.

60. The design for a new Congregational church in Week Street. The church was built in 1865/6 almost exactly as planned, even down to the finials on the corners of the building. It was a very typical classical building, designed for a prosperous commercial town congregation.

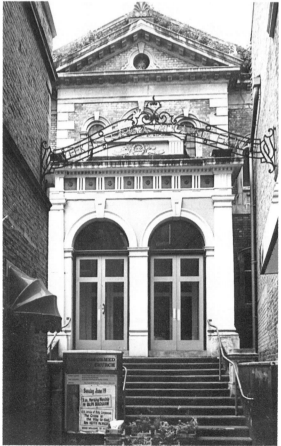

61. The Congregational church after the disastrous fire which gutted it. The finials and much of the entablature, however, survived.

62. The rebuilt Congregational church in 1988. It is in a small opening off the top of Week Street, lying back from the road between two shop premises. The church is now home for the town's United Reformed congregation.

63. The Methodist church in Union Street, dated 1823. A simple building with clean lines, original except for the modified porch.

64. The Salvation Army headquarters in Union Street, opposite the Methodist church.

Hospitals and Almshouses

spital, Maidstone.

65.   The West Kent General Hospital, *c.*1908. It was built in Marsham Street in 1832, the architect being John Whichcord, Senior. The building was much altered by Blandford 30 years later.

66. The Ophthalmic Hospital in Church Street opposite the now redundant Holy Trinity church. Once again, the local architect, Whichcord, is associated with the building, though he worked alongside Ashpital on this occasion. The hospital was built in 1852.

67. The Oakwood Hospital, dated 1830, also designed by John Whichcord, is entered through these most impressive lodges. The gateposts carry elaborate lamps with scroll feet.

68. After entering through the lodge gates, the visitor passes down the straight road flanked on both sides by rows of trees. At the far end is the main block, consisting of a central part of four storeys in a classical style, with three-storey wings extending on both sides. This is surely the grandest of all Whichcord's Maidstone buildings.

69. The modern part of the hospital is in marked contrast to its early Victorian origins. There are no elaborate entrance lodges or gates, just a large car park and direction signs instead of the impressive avenue of trees.

70.   The beautifully maintained Cutbush Almshouses. A plaque inside the entrance passage reads: 'The Cutbush Charity, 1867. Founded and endowed by Thomas Robert Cutbush in memory of his beloved brother Robert Cutbush'.

71. The layout of the Cutbush Almshouses is very traditional, with the buildings arranged round a central square of lawns and flower beds.

72. The Sir John Banks Almshouses in St Faith's Street. This is a fine brick building with a tiled roof, containing six living units. It was erected in 1700 and the plaque on the front reads: 'This almshouse was built in pursuance of the last will of Sir John Banks of Ailsford in ye county of Kent Baronet'.

The Medieval Group
from across the Medway

73. 'St Mary and All Saints College at Maidstone in Kent', *c.*1780. This print shows the area round the church and college, and the river bank, before it was commercially developed. The cart wheel tracks in the road, however, are evidence that the river was used for transportation of goods at that date.

74.   The view of the medieval buildings in 1818, showing the pastoral nature of the setting at that time. The water was obviously shallower than it is today.

75.   A view of the river and the medieval buildings, drawn by W. Bartlett in 1832. By that date the river was frequently used by small commercial sailing craft as land transport was so unreliable.

76. This view was drawn and engraved for Dugdale's *England and Wales Delineated* in the first half of the 19th century. The old bridge has long since been superseded and the distant view is now completely covered with buildings.

77. 'All Saints Church and College Maidstone. Engraved by J. Newman, 48 Watling Street, and drawn by A. Brothers.'

78. A 1987 photograph of the same view.

The Medieval Buildings around the Church

79. 'The Remains of the College at Maidstone, Kent, founded by Archbishop Courtney', an old print drawn by George Shepherd and engraved by J. Rogers in the early 19th century. This view is from the eastern end of All Saints' churchyard.

80. The 14th-century College from the north-east.

81. Exterior view of the gatehouse of the College, from the churchyard south-east of the church, *c.*1906. It is a three-storey building, with large and small entrance arches at the front. All the windows are under horizontal heads, those of the upper storey being transomed. The battlemented walls hide the eaves of the hipped roof.

82. A modern view of the inner, or southern, face of the gate tower of the College. Note that there is only a single entrance arch in this face, and windows only on the first storey. The material is the local Kentish ragstone.

83.   A modern view of what was the Master's House. It now houses the Kent Music School.

84.   This little road, between the College buildings and All Saints' church on the right, runs down to the river and no doubt formed the main entrance to both for heavy and bulky goods which were transported by water. The stone used to construct the buildings was probably unloaded here after being brought downstream from the quarries.

85.   The Archbishop's Palace, drawn by George Shepherd and published in 1829. Strictly speaking it was a manor house, the manor being the property of successive archbishops in medieval times. In 1348 John de Ufford, Archbishop-Elect, pulled down the old manor house and began to rebuild it, using material from the old Archbishop's Palace at Wrotham, but he died of the plague before he was consecrated and the work was completed by Archbishop Islip. Some additional work was done by Archbishop Courtenay in the last two decades of the 14th century. After the dissolution of the religious houses in the 16th century the property passed into lay hands, first to the Wyatt family and then to the Astleys. Early in the 17th century the Astleys added the present front, shown here, to the 14th-century building. In 1887 it was bought by public subscription for the Corporation in commemoration of Queen Victoria's jubilee.

86. A postcard of *c*.1906 showing the old Palace from across the river.

87. A modern view of the Archbishop's Palace.

88. A quiet walk between the old walls of the Palace and the river bank.

89. The gatehouse in front of the Palace is now the town's Information Centre. Its early use is obscure. It may have been a small private building, or perhaps more likely a water mill worked from the little River Len which runs immediately to the north of it. The gatehouse has several ancient windows, some lancets and others with 14th-century ogee heads.

90. The old stables, *c*.1905.

91. The Archbishop's stables, an interesting building with a projecting central front porch, timber-framed on the first storey, which now houses a Carriage Museum.

Breweries and Inns

92. The Medway Brewery, c.1970, viewed across the river in Fairmeadow. Brewing was recorded on this site as early as 1806. From that time the Brewery produced its own brand of beer, until 1956. It then brewed Courage beer until it was closed down in 1965. The building remained derelict until it was demolished in 1976.

93. The view across the river from Fairmeadow. The Brewery site is now being redeveloped. The church on the left is the old St Peter's, now redundant.

94. Fremlin's Brewery, *c.*1970, occupying the corner site where Earl Street meets Fairmeadow Street. Fremlin's were the largest Kent brewers but they were bought out by Whitbread in 1967. In 1976 the brewhouse was dismantled, and the fermenting block met the same fate five years later. The brewery has now been rebuilt and is used as a distribution centre.

95. The reconstructed yard of Fremlin's Brewery, now a major distribution centre.

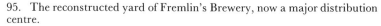

96. The *Royal Star Hotel* in the High Street, 1925. The *Royal Star* was an ancient inn which became an 18th-century coaching inn, an important stopping place for stage coaches which travelled through Maidstone on the roads from London, the Medway towns, and from the south and south-east of the county. Once the coaching age ended, it was a social centre where balls, celebration dinners and dances were held. It was also a rendezvous for the farmers, local businessmen and the gentry from the countryside when they came to town for the market or other business and social occasions. The hotel closed in 1985 and the building and its yard were converted into a shopping arcade.

97. The *Market House Inn* in Earl Street. It used to be called the *Coal Barge Inn* and its sign depicts one of the colliers which formerly brought coal from the North-East to Kent harbours and then up the River Medway to Maidstone.

98. Drakes Crab and Oyster Bar, with its triple gable ends facing forwards and an early gas lamp suspended from its front, is a surviving link with the past. The Martyrs' Plaque can be seen at the extreme right.

99.   The *Railway Hotel*, close to the West Station. In Victorian times, it would have provided accommodation for travellers and stables for horses. Before the age of the motor car, people would come into Maidstone on horseback or in horse-drawn vehicles, leave the animals in the care of the hotel's ostler, and then continue their journey by train.

100.   The front of the *Sun Inn* in Middle Row, a good example of a typical Kentish building style, with the second storey a little overhung at the front and with three equal gable ends facing forward. The *Sun* has been an inn since at least the 17th century.

101. An old house, an old roof, and some Kentish weatherboarding all combine to add charm to the rear of the old *Sun Inn*, facing into Bank Street.

Streets Old and New

102. The view down the High Street in 1829, drawn by George Shepherd.

103. A 19th-century view of the top of the High Street. The total wheeled traffic in this picture consists of one bicycle.

104. Another 19th-century view of the High Street.

105.   A Victorian drawing of the High Street. The horse cab stand just beyond the drinking fountain is now a taxi rank.

106.   The High Street in 1848, from a drawing by Mr. A. Brothers. It shows the *Red Lion Inn* on the right, Charles Dickens's inspiration for the *Blue Lion*, Muggleton, in *Pickwick Papers*.

107. The top part of the High Street, *c*.1908, with a tram at its stop by the drinking fountain.

108. The top of the High Street in 1988.

109. The town hall, built in 1762/3, as it appears in 1988. It was built both as a town hall and to accommodate the Western Division County Magistrates, who contributed £500 towards the cost of the building. The local M.P. also donated £300. The ground floor of the front is of ashlar, but the upper part is of brick laid in Flemish Bond. At the top of the centre section is a clock on a carved bracket. The roof is crowned by an open bell turret terminating in a wind vane.

110. An old photograph showing Middle Row in 1890.

111. Bank Street, to the rear of the town hall,
contains many fine old 17th- and 18th-century
buildings behind modern shop fronts.

112. No.18 Bank Street, a 17th-century four-
storey house with a double overhung front. The
pargeting depicts the royal arms and what are
believed to be the plumes of Prince Henry, son
of James I.

113. The west side of Mill Street in 1880. Most of these buildings have now disappeared.

114. Mill Street in the early years of the 20th century. Some road widening had to be carried out here, to accommodate the double tram tracks in the road, but horses and carts were still used to carry goods.

115.   The tram at its terminus in the Tonbridge Road, *c*.1906.

116.   Lower Stone Street, looking down the hill towards the Knightrider and Mote Road junction, *c*.1907. Note the horse-drawn carts and wagons, and the clothes worn by the children. This was, of course, a time of desperate poverty for many.

Important Buildings

117.   The Brotherhood Hall of the Corpus Christi fraternity. This old building in Earl Street is one of the town's surviving links with late medieval times. The plaque at the front reads: 'A non-monastic mediaeval religious guild of Maidstone men and women exercising most of the functions of a 19th. century friendly society existed here for over 200 years from A.D. 1422 to A.D. 1547. The hall with its cloisters was given to the Fraternity by John Hyssenden A.D. 1422. Receiving the royal charter of King Henry VI in 1441, the Fraternity was suppressed by King Henry VIII about the year 1547 and its property vested in the Crown.'
   A second plaque reads: 'The Maidstone Grammar School founded by the Corporation under royal charter of King Edward VI A.D. 1549 housed in these building for over 320 years was transferred to new larger premises in Tonbridge Road, Maidstone A.D. 1871. These buildings purchased from the Crown by the Corporation in 1548 for use as a grammar school were disposed of to private ownership on the transfer of the school to Tonbridge Road Maidstone in 1871.'

118.   The remains of the cloisters of the Corpus Christi fraternity, now used as a car park.

119.   The house in Earl Street, built by Andrew Broughton in the 17th century for his own use. He was twice mayor of Maidstone, a supporter of Parliament in the Civil War, and a leading figure in the town.

120. An early 20th-century photograph of the Mill Farm House on the corner of Knightrider Street and Lower Stone Street. It is a late 16th- or perhaps early 17th-century timber-framed house, the timbers having been hidden behind a coat of plaster applied in the 18th century, when plastered fronts were considered fashionable.

121. The old Mill House on the corner of Knightrider and Lower Stone Streets still survives, though now the 18th-century plaster has been removed, revealing the fine old timbered house in its original condition, a precious survival in a town which has lost so many of its good old buildings.

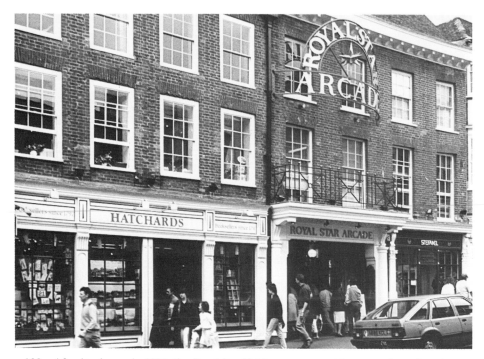

122.   After its closure in 1985, the *Royal Star Hotel* was converted into a modern shopping arcade.

123.   The bright and attractive interior of the Royal Star arcade.

124. The Kent Fire Office in the High Street, opposite the town hall, *c*.1906.

125. The Kent Fire Office in 1987, still an insurance headquarters.

126. Astley House in the High Street, built in 1587 and demolished in 1871.

127. A postcard of Astley House. This old building, one of several in the town which boasted pargeted fronts, mostly of the 17th century, has unfortunately not survived, and now only two such buildings remain.

128. This good 17th-century house in Bank Street has a shallow double overhang and, on the front of the first storey, four statues under crocketed ogee-headed windows. They represent four people who had some special impact upon the town: Archbishop Courtenay who established the College of Priests; Lawrence Washington an ancestor of the famous George Washington; William Caxton whose patron was Anthony Woodville, Earl Rivers, for whom Caxton produced the first book to be printed in Britain; and Lord Avebury.

129.   This building in Week Street, pargeted on its first and second floors, carries the date '1680' on the central panel of the first floor. On each side of the central panel are sash windows and, outside them, ornamental vases. The whole effect is most attractive and elegant.

130.   This good three-storey 18th-century house in Lower Stone Street, with its Venetian windows at first-storey level, is now divided into three units, of which the central one is No. 18. It is very typical of many such houses built at that time in Maidstone, but most have either been destroyed or much altered.

131. Tudor Cottage, one of the town's surviving old timber-framed houses, situated at the top of St Faith's Street, at the junction with Station Road.

132. The old Bluecoat School which was founded early in the 18th century and then occupied premises in the High Street, remaining there until the following century, when it moved into this building in Knightrider Street. The school survived until the last decade of the 19th century, and afterwards this old building was demolished, the site being used for the Baptist church which was completed in 1907.

133. Knightrider House in Knightrider Street, a clean cut, simple, three-storey 18th-century house, with a shallow hipped roof, once the home of William Shipley who died in 1803. The wall beside the entrance gate carries a plaque recording his occupancy.

134. This view, looking east from the end of Sandling Road, shows County Hall and, to the left, the *Wig and Gown* hotel and steakhouse, which was a favourite house of refreshment for legal gentlemen and others with engagements at County Hall. Sadly, the *Wig and Gown*, a distinguished building, has been demolished to make way for insurance offices.

135.   The *Wig and Gown* in its heyday in 1972.

136.   The insurance headquarters built at the town end of Sandling Road, on the site of the *Wig and Gown*.

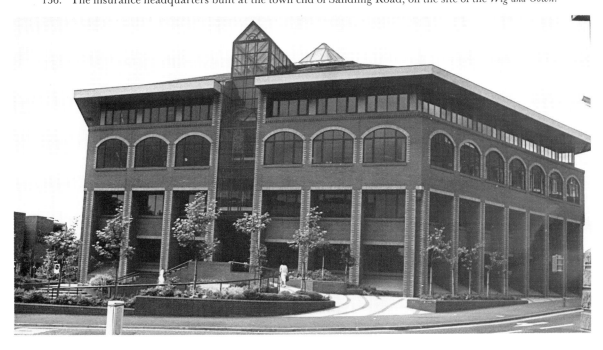

Memorials and Plaques

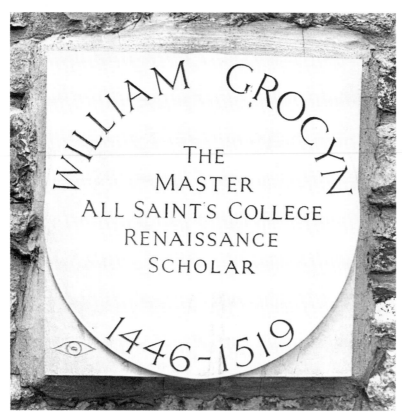

137. On the front of the Master's House, now the Kent Music School, is this reminder of William Grocyn, the famous renaissance scholar and humanist, and a friend of Erasmus, More, Colet and Linacre. He lectured at Exeter, Magdalen and New Colleges in Oxford, and at St Paul's in London, and also travelled and studied in Italy. He became master of All Saints' College, Maidstone, in 1506 at the age of 60, and died at the college in 1519 at the ripe old age of 73 years.

WILLIAM GROCYN
THE MASTER
ALL SAINTS COLLEGE
RENAISSANCE SCHOLAR
1446-1519

SEVEN PERSONS WERE BURNT · FOR THEIR FAITH · In 1557 near this spot

138. Affixed to the front of Drakes Crab and Oyster House is this sad sign, evidence of Maidstone's sacrifice in the dreadful religious persecution in the reign of Bloody Mary, 1553-58.

139. This plaque can be seen on the front of the substantial house in Earl Street built by Andrew Broughton who, like many local citizens, was a supporter of Parliament in the 17th-century Civil War. Since he was Clerk of the High Court of Justice he had the duty of reading Charles I's death sentence. He was a leading figure in the town, mayor twice, in 1648 and 1659, and he presented the town its much prized large mace.

140. William Shipley, founder of the Royal Society of Arts and one of the town's important sons, lies in this tomb between the north-west corner of the church of All Saints, and the old Palace.

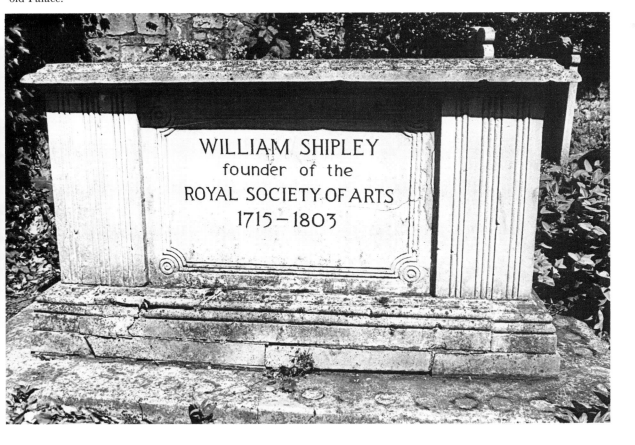

141.   A Victorian drawing captioned: 'The drinking fountain in Maidstone Market-place. Designed and executed by the late John Thomas'. On the plinth is a plaque which states: 'The gift of Alexr Randall to his native town 1862'.

142.   The drinking fountain at the top of the High Street was presented to the town by Alexander Randall, a successful Maidstone banker, senior partner of the New Kentish Bank which eventually became part of the present National Westminster Bank. The fountain, mounted on a substantial plinth in the form of a square base with a light at each corner, supports a statue of Queen Victoria under a canopy with a winged angel at each corner and surmounted by a crocketed pinnacle. It is said to be the last work of the sculptor John Thomas and was set up after his death, in about 1862. This area, the upper part of the High Street, is the site of the old market.

143. The war memorial in All Saints' churchyard, near the great east window.

Bridges

144. Maidstone's oldest bridge. This 13th-century bridge, now covered by Bishops Way, can be seen from a path beside the little river, just to the north of the present Information Offices. The Gothic pointed arches and the other stonework have been constructed in the local Kentish ragstone. This little bridge spans the River Len, which rises near the village of Lenham and flows into the River Medway about a hundred yards downstream from this bridge. For centuries the Len powered local watermills.

145. A very old drawing of the bridge over the Medway, published in 1787. It shows the one pointed arch in the centre, a feature shown in several pictures of this period. The water level is low, since the river was tidal until locks were constructed downstream.

146. This old print of the bridge was used by Hasted in his *History of Kent*, published in 1798.

147. A fine mid-19th-century view of old Maidstone Bridge. Left of the centre is the tower of All Saints' church. On the right hand bank of the river are warehouses and on the left timber is stacked on the wharf, waiting to be loaded on to ships.

148.   Maidstone Bridge, *c.*1860. This fine old bridge was considered unsafe by 1874. A new bridge was completed nearby in 1879 and this bridge was demolished soon afterwards. The sacks being transferred from the ship to the horse-drawn wagon probably contained corn or flour.

149. This three-span bridge was built in 1879, the successor to several others on approximately the same site from at least the 14th century. It was designed by Sir Joseph Bazalgette and has since been widened to carry additional traffic.

150. St Peter's Bridge, built in 1978, is a modern single-span construction, so blending in with its surroundings that it is not easily seen except from close at hand. Its construction, together with Bishops Way, has made possible one-way traffic across the river and relieved, to some extent, the town's perennial traffic problems.

Railway Stations

151. Although Maidstone was by-passed by the first main railway lines in Kent, it eventually acquired no fewer than three stations. This is Maidstone West, the earliest of the three, built by the South Eastern Railway to serve its extension from Paddock Wood in 1844. Unlike the other two stations it is a solid brick-built structure.

152. Maidstone East station was built when the London, Chatham and Dover Railway opened its line from Otford and then, ten years later, completed its extension to Ashford, thus providing a very direct line to the Channel ports. By this time, costly and elaborate station buildings were no longer being built and simple structures like this were the order of the day.

153. Maidstone Barracks station is a very modest construction, little more than a halt on the line from Maidstone West to Waterloo and Charing Cross.

Allington

154. Allington Castle, near the river bank on the northern side of Maidstone, was at first an earthen motte and bailey defensive work but it was destroyed in 1175 because it was built without planning permission! Henry II destroyed 'adulterine' castles, those built without Crown permission in the form of a 'Licence to Crenellate'. This was to prevent the subversion of royal authority by dissident barons. In 1279, however, one of the king's most trusted men, Sir Stephen de Pencester, did obtain a licence to crenellate here and built this lovely castle. Its purpose was twofold. It was to warn the people of Maidstone and the area to remain loyal to the king and, even more important, to defend Maidstone, the fertile valley of the Medway and the Weald from enemy invaders or bands of thieves. After the 16th century the castle became in turn a private residence, a farm and quarry, and finally a ruin before being bought by Sir Martin Conway and rebuilt at the start of the present century. It is now a religious house of the Carmelite order.

155.   Allington Castle in 1784, published in *The Antiquities of England and Wales*. At that time parts of the castle building were used as a farm and other parts were ruinous, the stone being used for buildings elsewhere.

156.   Allington Castle as a farm in 1822. The water shown is the wet moat outside the perimeter wall which was kept full by a stream from the nearby River Medway.

157. A 19th-century drawing of the dove house at Allington Castle. All large estates had at least one dove house, in which large flocks of pigeons were kept, their young, or squabs, providing a welcome supply of fresh meat at a time when most meat had to be salted.

158. The automatic flood control sluices at Allington. These electrically-operated sluices were opened in August 1937 by the Minister of Agriculture and Fisheries. They helped to alleviate Maidstone's flooding problems and keep the river at a constant level since the water above the sluices is no longer tidal.

159. The old lock-keeper's house beside the sluice gates and the lock at Allington in the early 20th century.

160. The Allington lock-keeper's house in 1987, in good condition but closed and unoccupied.

161. The old *Gibraltar Inn* as it appeared in the first half of the 19th century, when it was a favourite stopping-place for many a Victorian strolling along the river bank.

162. The famous *Malta Inn*, an old house of refreshment which is now a fashionable restaurant on the bank of the Medway near the sluices at Allington.

Mote Park

163.   Mote Park, the seat of Lord Romney, in 1783. This was the old house in Mote Park, demolished in 1801 after the present house was built.

164.   Mote Park in 1988: the view from the south-east. The modern fire escape, though necessary because the building is now a Cheshire Home, does nothing to improve the appearance of the late 18th-century building.

165. The pavilion in Mote Park was erected in 1801 by the Kent Volunteers to show their gratitude to Lord Romney for his hospitality to them at Mote Park when the Royal Review was held there in 1799. This print was published in 1812.

166. This print of Mote Park was published in 1821. This house, set in extensive grounds on the outskirts of the town, was designed by D. A. Alexander and built for Lord Romney, to replace an earlier house which previously stood there. Building commenced in 1793 and lasted for eight years. Below, in the valley, the water of the River Len was used to create a large lake. The house itself is now a Cheshire Home and 558 acres of the estate form a park, the property of the local authority.

167.   This view of Mote Park was both drawn and published by J. P. Neale.